FARRAR, STRAUS & GIROUX

NEW YORK

The Dhammapada

TRANSLATED FROM THE PALI BY P. Lal

To Isaac Bashevis Singer & Phil Ribet

without whose help in different ways this book could not have seen print

Copyright © 1967 by P. Lal. All rights reserved. Library of Congress catalog card
number: 67–13413. Published simultaneously in Canada by Ambassador Books, Ltd.,
Rexdale, Ontario. Designed by Marshall Lee. Printed in the United States of America.
First printing, 1967

PREFACE

This translation—in places at least, I hope, a transcreation—has a story behind it. Perhaps there is a moral in the story somewhere.

It happened in July 1966. I was in New York as an invited delegate from India to the XXXIVth International P.E.N. Congress. Glenway Wescott, with exceeding courtesy and hospitality, took it upon himself to introduce me to American writers and intellectuals. He gave a small cocktail party in the uptown Manhattan apartment of Monroe Wheeler, Director of the Museum of Modern Art, another unfailingly helpful and grace-imbued American. The others invited were Marianne Moore, Isaac Bashevis Singer and his wife, and Robert Phelps.

It was at the request of Miss Moore, who wanted to "hear some poetry from India," that I read out from my version of the *Dhammapada,* a few chapters of which I had in my briefcase. (Luckily, for ancient religious texts are not what one takes to cocktail parties.)

Miss Moore and the others were impressed by the Buddha's words, and Mr. Singer arranged to cable for the rest of the typescript to be airmailed from Calcutta. A contract was drawn up a week later by Mr. Robert Giroux, who has also helped by supplying friendly criticism and, whenever asked, by rushing Xerox copies of printed material hard to come across in India. The introduction could not have been written without his help.

I am grateful to Father Bayart, S.J., of St. Xavier's College, Calcutta, for allowing me the use of the excellent Oriental Collection in Goethals' Library; to Jai Ratan, for liking the first draft of this translation and thereby encouraging me to polish and improve; and to I. M. Rana, for typing the entire manuscript at very short notice.

P.L.

Calcutta
December, 1966

CONTENTS

SELECT BIBLIOGRAPHY

THE BUDDHA: HIS LIFE AND

HIS TEACHING

The Buddha

One of the many legends that circle around the Buddha's life says that his mother Maya left for her parents' house during the last days of her pregnancy, for this was the custom in India. On the way she asked her sister Prajapati to help her reach the flowering branch of a *sal* tree she had admired from her couch. As she reached for the branch, the tree bent graciously. Soft breezes blew in the scented forest. Her attendants hastily devised a curtain around her. She was still gazing with love at the beauty of the flowering bough when the Buddha was born, in springtime, on the full-moon day of the month of Vaisakh 563 B.C. His father was Raja Suddhodana. Maya and Prajapati were Suddhodana's wives. Maya was forty-five when the Buddha was born. He was named Siddhartha Gautama.

*

It was decreed that the nurse for Siddhartha, "the Blessing of the World," should be neither too tall, for in that case the neck of the infant would get strained; nor too short, for that would bend his body; nor too large, for that would constrict his legs; nor too weak, for that would not give his body the firmness it needed. Her breasts should not be too full, for then her hot milk would flush his skin; nor too dark, for then her milk would be cold, and cause hard and soft lumps on his growing body. After much searching, one hundred princesses were chosen.

*

Raja Suddhodana's Brahmin astrologer predicted that the special marks on Siddhartha's body indicated that he would forsake the world and become a Buddha.

"He will see the Four Visions—an old man, a diseased man, a dead man, and a holy man."

"Let such sights be forbidden in the palace," ordered Suddhodana.

*

Siddhartha was married to his beautiful cousin Yasodhara when he was sixteen. Three palaces—nine stories, seven stories, and five stories high—were built for their pleasure. Forty thousand dancing girls were provided for Siddhartha's delight. Nothing displeasing or offensive to the senses was brought before him.

*

One day in spring Siddhartha ordered his charioteer to take him to the royal pleasure gardens.

As the chariot, pulled by four resplendent horses, entered the gardens, Siddhartha saw an old bent man passing by.

> "Who is this, charioteer,
> Toothless, white-haired, tottering,
> Bones and nerves showing under skin?"

> "An old man, sire.
> He is weak and helpless.
> His friends and family have left him,
> As birds leave a withered tree."

"Tell me the truth, charioteer—
Did he become this himself,
Or does it happen to all?"

"Sire, this is the law of nature. It happens to all.
Men, women, and children grow old.
Your parents, your friends, you too will grow old."

Angry and disturbed, Siddhartha ordered the charioteer to
drive him back to the palace.

A few days later, not far from the spot where he had seen the
old man, he found a sick man abandoned beside a road.

"And this man, charioteer,
This skeleton, groaning in pain,
Fouled by his own filth?"

"A sick man, sire: he suffers,
There is no cure for him,
He will die soon."

Still later, he saw a procession of men carrying a body on a
coir cot.

"These men, charioteer, carrying
That man on a coir cot,
Disheveled, weeping, wailing . . . ?"

"Sire, the man is dead.
His parents, friends and relatives mourn.
He is no more in this world."

"So this is life! Youth into old age,
Health into disease.
Learned fools miscall it pleasure!"

Siddhartha locked himself up for many days in the palace.

When he went again to the pleasure gardens, he saw a monk passing by.

"Charioteer, this gracious man
In yellow garments, so serene
He never looks up—who is he?"

"A holy man, sire, a bhikku.
He has no desires, no possessions.
He looks on all with equal eyes."

"Good. He is a happy man.
The learned praise such a man.
I would like to be such a man."

For the first time he returned to his palace with a steady mind.

*

As he descended from his chariot, runners from his father greeted him with a message from the palace.

His wife Yasodhara had given birth to a son, and the message of his father was: "Announce my joy to my son."

Siddhartha listened, paused, and said:

"To me Rahula has been born." (Rahula in Sanskrit means "obstacle.") So the boy was named Rahula.

*

He entered the palace. A beautiful cousin, the virginal Kisha Gautami, saw him from an upper window and, struck by his handsome majesty, exclaimed:

> "Nibbhuta nuna samata
> Nibbhuta nuna sapita
> Nibbhuta nuna sanari
> Yasya yana i disa pati.
>
> Blessed the father
> Blessed the mother
> Blessed the wife
> Of a man so glorious!"

Siddhartha listened to the beautiful lines and wondered how he should achieve the state of blessedness (for *nibbhuta* meant both "fortunate" and "serene in Nirvana"). He unclasped a pearl necklace worth a hundred thousand gold coins, and sent it to her. When told it was for her, Kisha Gautami thought he had fallen in love with her.

*

Inside the palace, hundreds of elegantly dressed dancing and singing women, instructed by his father, surrounded him. Exquisite music and laughter, designed to chase away the loneliness of luxury, filled the rooms.

He looked at them and was not pleased. He closed his eyes and fell asleep.

They saw him sleeping. "If our lord sleeps, let us sleep too," they said to each other. Putting aside their kettledrums, vinas, finger bells, old flutes, and taking off their anklets, they slept.

He woke at midnight with a start. The oil-filled lamps were sputtering out. Around him he saw wild and violent women, some foaming at the mouth, some grinding their teeth, some mumbling, some yawning, some spitting, some drooling.

A room full of living corpses.

"Horrible! O horrible!" he whispered to himself.

He went quickly to the door, opened it, and shouted, "Anyone there?"

"I, Sire, Channa, keeper of the stables."

"Good Channa, saddle me a horse. I am leaving the palace tonight."

Outside the stables stood the magnificent steed Kantaka. His sleek black flanks glistened in the light of Channa's lamp. Saddling Kantaka, Channa brought him to the would-be Buddha.

*

In the meantime, Siddhartha went to the inner apartment of the palace where his wife Yasodhara was sleeping on a flower-strewn bed, her left hand resting lightly on the infant Rahula.

He stood at the door, silent, looking intently at mother and son, thinking.

Then, quickly, he went out to the courtyard, where Channa was waiting for him.

*

They rode to the bank of the river Aroma. Siddhartha asked Channa, who wept even as he obeyed, to inform his father, his mother, and his people that he had decided to become an ascetic.

"Tell them they must not feel sorry for me."

*

Siddhartha walked to Rajagriha, capital of Magadha, a city famous for its Brahmin sages and philosophers.

The king of Magadha, Bimbisara, informed by his guards about the arrival of a handsome and dignified mendicant in saffron (for Siddhartha had cut off his hair with his sword and exchanged his royal robe with a beggar), offered him wealth and invited him to stay in the palace.

Siddhartha declined and proceeded to the Magadhan hill where the wise men lived.

First he studied under Alara, the great Brahmin teacher. But Alara was learned only in the scriptures.

Next he went to Udraka. But Udraka was learned only in metaphysics.

*

He went to the forest of Uruvela near Bodh Gaya with five disciples, Kandanya, Bhaddaj, Mahanama, Vappa, and Assaji. There he joined the ascetics in severe self-mortification for six years.

He took food daily equal to the size of a sesamum seed. His flesh grew dark; his ribs showed; the thirty-two holy signs appeared on his body. One night, after the third watch, he collapsed.

A villager's daughter Sujata brought him food. He said later, "No food tasted better than the one brought to me by Sujata."

The ascetics knew only asceticism. Picking up his staff and begging bowl, he left them—and his five disciples, disillusioned, left him.

With Sujata's food in his hands, he sat down under the sacred *Bo*-tree. For he wanted to eat it undisturbed.

*

There he was assailed by Mara the temptress. "She came to me," he said later, "with these words:

> " 'Lean, suffering, ill-favored man,
> Live!
> Death is your neighbor.
> Death has a thousand hands,
> You have only two.
>   **Live!**

Live and do good
Live holy, and taste reward.
Why do you struggle?
Hard is struggle, hard to struggle all the time.' "

To which the holy Siddhartha replied:

"Why do you pick on me, Mara?
What will I do with goodness,
I who have faith?
            I struggle in faith, evil one,
            My faith is my life.
For look, my faith, like a burning wind
Drying up rivers,
            will dry up my blood,
            will dry up everything that flows.
Till blood, bile, and phlegm dry up,
I shall sit here,
            with tranquil mind,
            and steady wisdom.

Faith is my weapon. Powerless
Against it is your army, O temptress.
Bring Lust and Restlessness,
Hunger and Thirst,
Sloth, Cowardice, Doubt, Hypocrisy—
All powerless."

He sat under the *Bo*-tree, unmoved, while Mara assailed him incessantly. Around him danced a host of fierce soldiers, with spears, swords, clubs, and diamond maces. They had heads of hogs, of fish, asses, horses, snakes, tigers, and dragons. Some had one eye only, others many. They flew and leapt, striking at each other, howling and hooting and whining till the earth shook. The earth shook like a loving bride abducted from her husband.

*

That evening, from sunset onwards, till the next dawn, wisdom slowly came to Siddhartha. He achieved Nirvana at dawn, and as the full experience of truth flashed on him, he exclaimed:

"Anekajati samsaram
sandha isman anibhisam
gahakarakanga visanta
dukhayati punah punam . . .

How many births have I known
Without knowing the builder of this body!
How many births have I looked for him.
It is painful to be born again and again.

But now I have seen you, O builder of this body!
All desire is extinct, Nirvana is attained!
The rafters have crumbled, the ridgepole is smashed!
You will not build them again."

He was now the Buddha.

*

A voice inside him kept repeating:

> "Why reveal to the world
>   your hard-won truth?
> Can the lustful and selfish
>   ever grasp this truth?
>
> Inexplicable and profound
>   is the truth now yours;
> How can he know it
>   whose mind is full of the world?"

But the Buddha rose like a lotus from stagnant water whose petals are unsullied by muddy drops, and saw the world clearly, with a Buddha's serene eyes. He saw the pure men, and the impure, the noble and the ignoble, the good listeners and the wicked ones, the seekers of immortality and those contemptuous of it.

*

And he was moved to pity.

> Because he saw mankind drowning in the sea of *samsara,* of birth, death, and sorrow,
> And because there stirred in his heart the desire to save them,
>   He was moved to pity.
> Because he saw them lost in false doctrine, with none to guide them,

And because they wallowed in the five lusts, and suffered,
      He was moved to pity.
Because they clung to their wealth, their wives, and their children,
And because they did not know how to leave them, though they
    wanted to leave them,
      He was moved to pity.
Because he saw them afraid of birth, old age, and death,
And because they continued to act in ways that brought birth, old
    age, and death,
      He was moved to pity.
Because it was a time of war and pestilence, killing and maiming,
And because they had hatred in their hearts, for which they would
    suffer,
      He was moved to pity.
Because some were rich, and clung to riches,
Because some were born, and would not find the Dhamma,
Because some plowed and sowed, and bought and sold,
And the fruit they reaped was the bitter one of suffering,
      He was moved to pity.

His Teaching

"You who follow me, consider this carefully. Keep an eye open, seekers of truth. Weigh rumor, custom, and hearsay. Don't let anyone's excellence in the Scriptures mislead you. Logic and argument, supply of elaborate reasons, approval of considered opinion, plausibility of ideas, respect for the leader who guides you—beware of too much trust in them. Only when you *know,* and are sure that you know—this is not good, this is erroneous, this is censured by the intelligent, this will lead to loss and grief—only when you know, should you reject or accept it."

*

When the Enlightened One was staying at Kosambi, in the Simsapa Grove, he took up a fistful of *simsapa* leaves and turned to his followers.

"What do you think, friends? Are there more *simsapa* leaves in my hand than in the *simsapa* grove?"

"Very few in your hand, lord; many more in the grove."

"Exactly. So you see, friends, the things that I know and have not revealed are more than the truths I know and have revealed.

"And why have I not revealed them?

"Because, friends, there is no profit in them; because they are not helpful to holiness; because they do not lead from disgust to cessation and peace, because they do not lead from knowledge to wisdom and Nirvana.

"That is why I have not revealed them."

*

"I will teach you Dhamma. Here is Dhamma: if *this* is, *that* also is; if *this* is reborn, *that* is reborn; if *this* is not, *that* also is not; when *this* stops, *that* stops too."

*

"No matter whose the teachings, my friend, if you are sure of this —'These doctrines conduce to passion, not serenity; bondage, not freedom; increase, not loss, of material gain; greed, not thrift; restlessness, not calm; noisy company, not solitude; sloth, not energy; delight in evil, not performance of good'—well, rest assured that is not the Dhamma, that is not the Discipline, that is not the Master's Way.

"But if there are teachings, no matter whose, you are sure will conduce to serenity, not passion; freedom, not bondage; loss, not increase, of material gain; thrift, not greed; calm, not restlessness; solitude, not noisy company; energy, not sloth; performance of good, not delight in evil—that is the Dhamma, that is the Discipline, that is the Master's Way."

*

"The ocean has only one taste, the taste of salt. Dhamma has only one taste, the taste of Nirvana."

*

"Consider, Malunkyaputta, this story of a man wounded by a poisoned arrow. His friends, relatives, and well-wishers gather around him and a surgeon is called. But the wounded man says, 'Before he takes out this arrow, I want to know if the man who shot me was a Kshatriya, a Brahmin, a merchant, or an untouchable.'

"Or he says, 'I won't let this arrow be removed until I know the name and tribe of the man who shot me.'

"Or: 'Was he tall, short, or of medium height?'

"Or: 'Was he black, brown, or yellow-skinned?'

"What do you think would happen to such a man, Malunkyaputta? Let me tell you. He will die.

"And that is what happens when a man comes to me and says, 'I will not follow the Dhamma until the Buddha tells me whether the world is eternal or not eternal, whether the world is finite or infinite, whether the soul and the body are the same or different, whether the liberated person exists or does not exist after death, or both exists and does not exist after death, whether he neither exists nor does not exist after death.' He will die, Malunkyaputta, before I get a chance to make everything clear to him.

"Being religious and following Dhamma has nothing to do with the dogma that the world is eternal; and it has nothing to do with the other dogma that the world is not eternal. For whether the world is eternal or otherwise, birth, old age, death, sorrow, pain, misery, grief, and despair exist. I am concerned with the extinction of these.

"Therefore, consider carefully, Malunkyaputta, the things that I have taught and the things that I have not taught. What are the things I have not taught?

"I have not taught that the world is eternal. I have not taught that the world is not eternal. I have not taught that the world is finite. I have not taught that the world is infinite. I have not taught that the soul and the body are the same. I have not taught that the soul and the body are different. I have not taught that the liberated person exists after death. I have not taught that he does not exist after death. I have not taught that he both exists and does not exist after death; that he neither exists nor does not exist after death.

"Why, Malunkyaputta, have I not taught all this? Because all this is useless, it has nothing to do with real Dhamma, it does not lead to cessation of passion, to peace, to supreme wisdom, and the holy life, to Nirvana. That is why I have not taught all this.

"And what have I taught, Malunkyaputta? I have taught that suffering exists, that suffering has an origin, that suffering can be ended, that there is a way to end suffering.

"Why, Malunkyaputta, have I taught this? Because this is useful, it has to do with real Dhamma, it leads to the cessation of passion, it brings peace, supreme wisdom, the holy life, and Nirvana. That is why I have taught all this.

"Therefore, Malunkyaputta, consider carefully what I have taught and what I have not taught."

＊

"Tell me, O Enlightened One, is there a Self?"

The Buddha kept silent.

"Is there, then, no Self?"

He did not reply.

Vacchagotta rose and left. The noble Ananda asked the Buddha, "Why, lord, did you not answer Vacchagotta's questions?"

"Supposing, Ananda, I had replied that there is a Self; that would have meant siding with those ascetics and Brahmins who describe themselves as Eternalists. If I had replied there is no Self, that, Ananda, would have meant siding with those ascetics and Brahmins who class themselves as Annihilationists. I have constantly held that all things are not-Self—would it have been right on my part then to have told Vacchagotta that there *is* a Self? And if I had replied that there is not a Self, wouldn't this have confused him even more? He would have gone away saying to himself, 'I believed in a Self. What is there left for me now?'"

*

"All things, O monks, are on fire. And what are these things which are on fire?

"The eye is on fire. Things seen are on fire. Eye vision is on fire. Impressions received by the eye are on fire. Whatever sensation, pleasant or unpleasant, is connected with the eye, is on fire.

"With what are these on fire?

"With the fire of desire, with the fire of hate and delusion; with birth, old age, death, sorrow, lamentation, misery, grief, and despair.

"All things are burning.

"The ear is on fire; sounds are on fire . . . The nose is on fire; odors are on fire . . . The tongue is on fire; tastes are on fire . . . The body is on fire; things touched are on fire . . . The mind is on fire; ideas are on fire . . . Mind-awareness is on fire; impressions received by the mind are on fire . . . whatever sensation, pleasant or unpleasant, is connected with the mind is also on fire . . .

"With what are these on fire?

"With the fire of desire, with the fire of hate and delusion; with birth, old age, death, sorrow, lamentation, misery, grief, and despair.

"All things are burning.

"Cultivate aversion, O monks, and be free of the fire of desire . . ."

*

"Avoid these two extremes, monks. Which two? On the one hand, low, vulgar, ignoble, and useless indulgence in passion and luxury; on the other, painful, ignoble, and useless practice of self-torture and mortification. Take the Middle Path advised by the Buddha, for it leads to insight and peace, wisdom and enlightenment, and to Nirvana.

"What, you will ask me, is the Middle Path? It is the Eightfold Way. Right views, right intentions, right speech, right action, right profession, right effort, right watchfulness, right concentration. This is the Middle Path, which leads to insight, peace, wisdom, enlightenment, and Nirvana.

"For there is suffering, and this is the noble truth of suffering
—birth is painful, old age is painful, sickness is painful, death is
painful; lamentation, dejection, and despair are painful. Contact
with the unpleasant is painful, not getting what you want is
painful.

"Suffering has an origin, and this is the noble truth of the
origin of suffering—desire creates sorrow, desire mixed with pleasure and lust, quick pleasure, desire for life, and desire even for
non-life.

"Suffering has an end, and this is the noble truth of the end
of suffering—nothing remains of desire, Nirvana is attained, all is
given up, renounced, detached, and abandoned.

"And this is the noble truth that leads to Nirvana—it is the
Eightfold Way or right views, right intentions, right speech, right
action, right profession, right watchfulness, and right concentration.

"This is the noble truth of suffering. This must be understood."

*

"I do not quarrel with the world, monks; it is the world that
quarrels with me. How can a true disciple of Dhamma quarrel
with the world? If the learned are agreed that a thing is, I agree
with the learned that it is. If the learned are agreed that it is not,
I agree with the learned that it is not.

"What are the learned agreed upon as 'It is not'? The material world is permanent, stable, eternal, unchanging—they are agreed that this is not so. I agree with them that this is not so. And the same applies to feeling, perception, consciousness, and thought structure.

"What are the learned agreed upon as 'It is'? The material world is impermanent, unstable, changing, and full of suffering— they are agreed that this is so. I agree with them that this is so. And the same applies to feeling, perception, consciousness, and thought structure . . .

"Just as a blue, red, or white lotus grows in stagnant water, but rises clear and unpolluted out of it, a truth-finder grows up in the world but overcomes it, and is not soiled by it."

*

"Look, Assalayana, Brahmin women have periods, conceive, give birth, and breast feed their children. And yet these Brahmins, born as all other children are born, say that they are better than children from the other castes . . .

"What do *you* think, Assalayana? Is only a Brahmin capable of having a heart of gold, can only a Brahmin show love, gentleness, and goodness? Can't a warrior, a merchant, a worker? . . . Can only a Brahmin go to the river with a string of bath balls and powder and wash himself clean of dirt? Can't a warrior, a merchant, a worker? Is the fire produced by a Brahmin rubbing two *sal* sticks together any brighter than the fire produced by a trapper, bamboo weaver, or scavenger who picks up two sticks from a pig-sty or dog trough?"

*

A village chief came to the Buddha and asked:

"Is the Buddha compassionate to all living creatures, big and small?"

"Yes," he replied.

"Then why does the Buddha teach Dhamma in full to some and not to others?"

"A good question. Tell me, village chief, supposing a farmer had three fields, one fertile, one average, and one rocky—when the time came to sow seed, which would he sow first?"

"First the fertile, then the average, then perhaps the rocky one, because that would not even give him cattle fodder."

The Buddha said, "For the same reason, I teach Dhamma in full, in beginning, middle, and end, in spirit and in letter, to the monks and nuns first . . . Then I teach it to the lay followers . . . Then the others."

*

"Take a physician skilled in his science, a learned and humane person. He has many sons—let us say ten, or twenty, or, if you like, a hundred. He is called to some important business in a foreign land; in his absence his sons take some harmful drugs, which send them rolling on the ground in fever and frenzy. He returns just in time, and what does he find? Some are beyond cure; others are still in their senses. These welcome him and kneeling before him say, 'How good for us that you have returned in time! We were fools. We didn't know the drugs were so poisonous. Please make us well again.'

"The father is moved by their suffering and selects some fine plants and herbs, delicately flavored and colored. He pounds, sifts, and mixes them in the right proportions and gives the medicine to them, saying, 'This is good medicine. Take it: it is delicately flavored and colored. It will cure you of your suffering.'

"The sensible ones see quickly the truth of his words, take the medicine, and are cured.

"The others are happy too that their father is back and ask him to heal their illness, but when the medicine is offered, they refuse it. Why? Because the drugs they have taken have confused their power of judgment, and they are not sure if this excellent medicine is really as excellent as claimed.

"So the father thinks to himself: 'What a pity they cannot see straight. They are glad to see me back but are unwilling to take the medicine I give them. Let me see what can be done.'

"He tells them, 'I am an old man, I haven't long to live. I must make preparations to leave this world. I leave behind this medicine. Keep it with you. It won't lose its power to heal.' So he goes away to a foreign land and sends a messenger to them with this news: 'Your father is dead.'

"The news shocks them. 'Our father is dead,' they whisper

among themselves. 'If he were living, he would give us the right medicine. He would cure us. But he has died in a foreign land.'

"They are grief-stricken, and their grief soon opens their eyes. Now they see the value of the delicately flavored and colored medicine their father gave them before he left. They quickly take it and are cured. When the news reaches their father that they are cured, he returns.

"Tell me, my friends, what do *you* think? Who is there among you who will condemn the good physician for telling a lie?"

*

They called her Kisha Gautami, the "Frail" Gautami, because she was delicate and tired easily. She had sung the song heard by the young would-be Buddha as he entered the palace; she had received the necklace he had sent her, and thought he was in love with her. Then she had died, quickly and suddenly. She was reborn as Kisha Gautami in the house of poor people in the city of Savatthi. They married her off early because her husband's people were well-off.

But because she came of poor parents, her in-laws neglected her; they would even mock her. When she gave birth to a son, they stopped neglecting and mocking her. For the first time she knew what it was to be respected.

The boy grew up and reached the age when he could play and run about with friends. Then, quietly and suddenly, he died.

Kisha felt a deep pain inside her. "They respected me because

I gave birth to him. What will they do to me now? What will they do to him? They will throw his body away."

She placed her dead son on her left hip and went from house to house, saying, "Give my son medicine. Bring my son back to me."

They laughed. *Medicine for the dead?* They clapped their hands and made fun of her. *What do you mean? You must be mad.*

A wise man saw her and said to himself, "If there is any medicine to be had for a person in such a condition, it will be found with the Buddha."

So he said to her, "Good woman, go to the Tathagatha, the one who has reached what has to be reached. There is none greater than him in the world of men and the world of gods. Go to the monastery where he meditates. Ask him for medicine." With her son on her left hip, she went and stood on the outside of the crowd that had gathered around the Buddha.

"O holy one," she said loudly, "give me medicine for my son!"

He looked at her.

"You did well, Kisha Gautami," he replied, "in coming here for medicine. Listen to me carefully. Go back to the city, begin at the beginning, and bring me a fistful of mustard seed from the first house in which no one has ever died."

"I will do so, holy one," she said gratefully.

Joyfully she entered the first house and said, "The holy one wants me to bring him a fistful of mustard seed as medicine for my son. Can you give me mustard seed?"

They brought out and gave her mustard seed.

"Has anyone died in this house?" she asked.

"They have never stopped dying," they replied. "So many deaths . . ."

"Take back the seed," Kisha Gautami said. "The holy one told me not to bring mustard seed from a house in which a death had taken place."

"Poor Gautami," they said, "the dead are everywhere."

She went to a second house—to a third—and a fourth. There must be *one* without a death in it! The Buddha could not have been so cruel. He would have had some pity on her.

She could not find a single house to bring mustard seed from.

She took her son to the cremation ground, holding him in front of her in her arms.

"O my son, my little son, my dear son," she said, "I thought when you died, only you died. But death is everywhere. It is a universal law—all must die. Village law, market law, house law are passing; only this law is eternal." She placed her child on the cremation ground and went back to the Buddha.

"Kisha Gautami," he asked, "did you get the mustard seed?"

"Holy one," she replied, "enough of this business of the mustard seed! Only give me refuge."

*

"Monks, listen to the parable of the raft. A man going on a journey sees ahead of him a vast stretch of water. There is no boat within sight, and no bridge. To escape from the dangers of this side of the bank, he builds a raft for himself out of grass, sticks, and branches. When he crosses over, he realizes how useful the raft has been to him and wonders if he should not lift it on his shoulders and take it away with him. If he did this, would he be doing what he should do?"

"No."

"Or, when he has crossed over to safety, should he keep it back for someone else to use, and leave it, therefore, on dry and high ground? This is the way I have taught Dhamma, for crossing, not for keeping. Cast aside even right states of mind, monks, let alone wrong ones, and remember to leave the raft behind."

*

"Take the case of the raja of Savatthi. He ordered a man to assemble all the blind subjects of the kingdom and bring an elephant in front of them.

"This was done. The man said to the assembled group: 'This is an elephant.' He let one feel the elephant's head, another its ear, still another its tusk; and so on until the trunk, foot, back, tail and tail tuft were covered. To each who felt, he said, 'This is an elephant.'

"The raja turned to his blind subjects and asked them, one by one, what they thought an elephant was. The head feeler thought an elephant was a pot. The ear feeler was convinced it was a winnowing basket. The tusk became a plowshare, the trunk a plow, the foot a pillar, the tail a whip, and the tuft a floor duster.

"And they quarreled, shouting, 'I know what an elephant is!' 'No, I do!' 'You're wrong!' 'It's like this!' They came to blows. The raja was pleased, for he had made his point.

"So you see, monks, how the sects quarrel over Dhamma, each thinking it has the full truth. They are blind, they do not know, they do not see the goal."

*

"The noble Eightfold Way arises by living with what is lovely. If already risen, it grows to perfection by constant friendship with what is lovely."

*

"He picked up a flower and showed it to the assembled people.

"They did not understand. Only Mahakashyapa smiled.

" 'I have in my hand,' he said, 'the doctrine of the right Dhamma, birthless, deathless, formless, inscrutable. It is beyond sacred texts; it does not need words to explain it. I give it to Mahakashyapa.' "

*

"This must be your motto, monks: No shrinking back, no giving up the struggle, only the going forward. Always have this thought in your mind: 'Let me be reduced to skin and bone, and let my flesh and blood dry up; so long as I have a glimmer of energy I will not give up the search for truth.' This must be the way you train yourselves."

*

"I am now eighty years old, Ananda. The end of my journey has come. I drag my body along like a worn-out bullock cart, with great hardship.

"It is only when my thoughts are completely concentrated on the inner vision that has no bodily object that my body is at peace.

"Therefore, Ananda, be a lamp to yourself. Be an island. Learn to look after yourself; do not wait for outside help.

"Hold fast to the truth as a lamp. Be an island. Only truth can save you. Do not look for any help besides yourself.

"How is this to be done, Ananda? How is one to be a lamp to oneself and not wait for outside help, hold fast to the truth, and seek Nirvana in the truth? How is one to be an island?

"Let a man, though living in the body, so treat his body that, with right effort, right watchfulness, and right concentration, he will overcome the sorrow that is produced by the sensations that arise in the body . . .

"Whoever, now or after I die, shall be a lamp to himself, an island to himself, and shall not look outside of himself for refuge —he alone, Ananda, shall attain what is important to be attained. But he must make the effort himself . . .

"No, Ananda, no weeping. How often have I told you that

it is in the very nature of life that what we love most must be taken from us? How can it be otherwise? What is born is doomed at the moment of its birth to die. There is no other way.

"Some of you will say, 'The Teacher is no more, we have no one left to lead us.' But is not the Dhamma with you, and the Sangha? Have I not left these behind? Let them be your Teachers.

"One last word, bhikkus. Whatever consists of component parts will die. Work out your Nirvana with diligence."

*

King Milinda asked: "Have you, respected Nagasena, seen the Buddha?"

"No, sire," replied the philosopher Nagasena.

"Did your gurus see him?"

"No, sire."

"Well, what if I say then that there is no such person as the Buddha?"

"Sire, have you seen the Himalayan river Uha?"

"No, Nagasena."

"Did your father ever see it?"

"Not that I know."

"Then there is no such river as the Uha."

"But there is, Nagasena. I may not have seen it and my father may not have seen it, but there is a river called Uha."

"So, sire: I may not have seen him, and my gurus may not have seen him, but there is such a person as the Buddha."

"Good, holy Nagasena. But is the Buddha greater than all?"

"Yes, sire."

"But you have not seen him, Nagasena. How do you know he is greater than all?"

"Let me explain, sire. Could those who have not seen the great ocean declare it to be powerful, deep, and immeasurable? Could they pronounce its fullness unaffected though the five great rivers Ganga, Yamuna, Achiravati, Sorabhu, and Mahu, flow into it all the time?"

"Yes, they could."

"So could I, sire, have seen great disciples who have attained Nirvana declare that the Buddha is greater than all."

"But where is the Buddha? Here or there?"

"Neither here nor there, sire."

"What do you mean, respected Nagasena?"

"Supposing, sire, the flames of a great fire are extinguished, where do they go? Here or there? Where?"

"Neither here nor there. They disappear."

"So, when the Buddha achieved Nirvana, sire, he became neither here nor there. But you may know him by the Dhamma, for he taught the Dhamma, and left it behind."

THE DHAMMAPADA

Ten Twin Verses

We are what we think,
having become what we thought.
Like the wheel that follows the cart-pulling ox,
Sorrow follows an evil thought.

And joy follows a pure thought,
like a shadow faithfully tailing a man.
We are what we think,
having become what we thought.

How will hate leave him if a man forever thinks,
"He abused me, he hit me, he defeated me, he robbed me"?

Will hate ever touch him if he does *not* think,
"He abused me, he hit me, he defeated me, he robbed me"?

There is only one eternal law:
Hate never destroys hate; only love does.

Some never see the point of disciplining themselves.
Others do; they are the wise ones; they do not argue.

How quickly does a small tree break before a big wind!
So Mara the temptress breaks all who are
        lascivious, restless, gluttonous, and slothful.

Impossible for the wind to bend a mountain!
So is Mara helpless before all who are
    moderate, disciplined, full of faith, and active.

What good is a yellow robe if your mind is not pure?
What will the robe do, if truth is lacking, discipline is denied?

Cast aside meanness, stand on virtue,
learn discipline and speak the truth.
Then will the robe fit you.

Foolish to think that truth is in untruth,
equally foolish that untruth is in truth—
such thinking leads nowhere.

Truth is always truth,
untruth always untruth—
this is what matters, this is right desire.

Like rain seeping through an ill-thatched hut,
passion enters the careless mind.

Passion surrenders to the careful mind
like rain helpless before a well-thatched hut.

Only suffering for the evil man—
suffering now, suffering later,
suffering in this world and the next.
His deeds breed suffering, and he suffers.

Happiness for the good man—
happiness now, happiness later,
happiness in this world and the next.
His deeds breed happiness, and he rejoices.

For the evil man, suffering now and later,
suffering everywhere.
"I have done wrong," he says—and suffers, now.
More suffering for him in the next birth.

For the good man, happiness now and later,
happiness everywhere.
"I have done good," he says—and rejoices.
He rejoices more in the next birth.

Lazy cowherd counting others' cows,
having none of his own,
what good is parroting of holy texts
if a man will not get up and gather holiness?

Words do not matter; what matters is Dhamma.
What matters is action rightly performed,
after lust, hate, and folly are abandoned,
with true knowledge and serene mind,
and complete detachment from the fruit of action.

Clear Thinking

Clear thinking leads to Nirvana,
a confused mind is a place of death.
Clear thinkers do not die,
the confused ones have never lived.

The wise man appreciates clear thinking,
delights in its purity, and
selects it as the means to Nirvana.

He meditates, he perseveres,
he works hard for the incomparable freedom and bliss of Nirvana.

He steps forward:
this clear thinker and pure worker,
this dignified and disciplined disciple of Dhamma.

Clear thinking, right action, discipline and restraint
make an island for the wise man,
an island safe from floods.

Sloth is loved by the ignorant and foolish;
the wise man's treasure is his clear thinking.

"Never sloth, never lust, never the senses"—
This is clear thinking, which brings great joy.

Suppressing sloth steadily, slowly,
a man climbs the tower of serene wisdom.
Sees, below, the suffering multitudes,
as one from a high hill sees the level plain.

While others sleep he is awake,
they sleep, he works.
He is the wise man,
    the race horse swiftly advancing.

Clear thinking made Indra chief god.
Let us praise clear thinking, confusion canceler.

For it moves like a flame, burning
all bondage, big and small.
A bhikku with clear thinking sees confusion clearly,
    and is not afraid.

A bhikku with clear thinking is close to Nirvana.
He sees confusion clearly, and is not afraid.

Mind

Like an archer an arrow,
the wise man steadies his trembling mind,
    a fickle and restless weapon.

Flapping like a fish thrown on dry ground,
it trembles all day, struggling
    to escape from the snares of Mara the temptress.

The mind is restless.
To control it is good.
A disciplined mind is the road to Nirvana.

Look to your mind, wise man;
look to it well—it is subtle, invisible, treacherous.
A disciplined mind is the road to Nirvana.

Swift, single, nebulous,
it sits in the cave of the heart.
Who conquers it, frees himself from the slavery of death.

No point calling him wise
whose mind is unsteady,
who is not serene,
who does not know the Dhamma.

Call him wise
whose mind is calm,
whose senses are controlled,
who is unaffected by good and evil,
who is wakeful.

He knows the body for what it is,
                              a frail jar;
he makes his mind firm
                              like a fortress.
He attacks Mara with
                              the weapon of wisdom,
he guards what he conquers
                              jealously.

It is not long before the body,
                              bereft of breath and feeling,
lies on the ground, poor thing,
                              like a burnt-out faggot.

No hate can hurt, no foe can harm,
as hurts and harms a mind ill disciplined.

Neither father, mother, nor relative can help
as helps a mind that is well disciplined.

Flowers

Who conquers this world,
      the world of Yama and the world of the gods?
Like a connoisseur picking a flower,
      the good man chooses Dhamma.

The good man conquers this world,
      the world of Yama and the world of the gods.
He is the connoisseur picking a flower,
      the disciple of Dhamma.

Knowing flesh is only froth,
      like a dream in a desert,
      the disciple transcends
      the flowery arrows of lust.
Death cannot touch him.

Like floods that come and collect an unsuspecting village,
death claims the restless collector of flowers.

His mind is restless
      after many flowers,
before he can have them
      death is upon him.

Let the wise man live
      in the flower of his village,
like the bee, gently taking honey,
      but harming neither color nor scent.

It is not what others do,
      or do not do, that is my concern:
It is what I do,
      and what I do not do, *that* is my concern.

Lovely flowers without fragrance
Are sweet words without sweet action.

Lovely flowers full of fragrance
Are sweet words with sweet action.

Is there a limit to the variety of garlands
      skilled hands make from a heap of flowers?
Is there a limit to the number of good deeds
      a man may do once he is born?

The wind carries the scent of flowers only where it goes,
      sandalwood, jasmine, and *tagara* fragrance,
but the fragrance of good men spreads everywhere,
      their fame is endless.

Sandalwood and *tagara* are delicately scented,
      and give a little fragrance,
but the fragrance of virtue
      rises even to the gods.

And Mara stands helpless
before the clear thinker and perfect knower,
the good man.

Like the lotus softly fragrant and
      soul-delighting,
rising clear from scraps of rubbish in
      a wayside pond,

The disciple of the Enlightened Buddha shines
      in perfect wisdom
Clear above the crowds of ordinary men
      who do not see the truth.

The Fool

Very long is the night to him who is awake,
very long the road to him who is weary,
very long is life to the fool without Dhamma.

If you find no better or equal on life's road,
go alone!
Loneliness is better than friendship of a fool.

"These sons are mine.
This wealth is mine."
The words of a fool.
He himself is not his.
How can sons be his?
How can wealth be his?

The fool who knows he is foolish is, let us say, wise,
The fool who thinks he is wise is hugely foolish.

Does a spoon know the taste of broth?
Can a fool learn wisdom from a pandit?

As quickly as a tongue knows the taste of broth,
a serious man learns wisdom from a pandit.

A fool is his own enemy,
does evil deeds, reaps bitter fruit.

Ill done is deed that breeds bitterness,
whose reward is lamentation and remorse.

Well done is deed that gives sweetness,
whose reward is unending delight.

Ill deed is sweet—so the fool thinks.
Till it bear fruit—which is bitterness and grief.

A fool sits with a blade of holy grass,
        with which he daily licks a pot of honey,
yet his holiness is not one-sixteenth
        that of the wise knower of Dhamma.

Fresh milk does not curdle,
        neither does a fresh evil deed;
like embers under ashes, it smolders,
        and slowly destroys the fool.

The little knowledge a fool picks up
        goes against him,
his share of brightness gets tarnished,
        his merit is destroyed.

What a fool wants is cheap fame,
lordship over bhikkus, power in monasteries,
and puja from everybody.

"Look, householder, look, monk,
I do this, I am powerful,
I know what's right and I know what's wrong."
The pride and passion of a fool's words!

One road goes to profit, another to Nirvana.
Know this, O bhikku, disciple of Buddha,
and struggle for wisdom, not the world's fame.

The Wise Man

If a pandit rebukes or advises,
follow him—
he is a wise man, a revealer of hidden treasures.
Only good can come from him.

If he instructs, restrains, or commands,
follow him, as the right-minded do.
The ill-minded do not care.

Choose friends virtuous and excellent.
Shun the low-minded and ill-doing.

To drink Dhamma is to be serene.
Wisdom finds delight in the noble Dhamma.

Planners make canals,
archers shoot arrows,
craftsmen fashion woodwork,
the wise man molds himself.

Wind will not move rock,
nor praise and blame a wise man.

The words of the Dhamma flow into him:
he is clear and peaceful like a lake.

Good men do not stop working.
Good men do not gossip, good men are undemanding.
Joy does not affect them, nor sorrow.
Good men are constant.

A man who does not want
a son, a kingdom, or money
for himself or for others,
a man who uses prudence
in furthering his own welfare—
such a man is holy,
such a man is wise and virtuous.

Most wander lost here,
very few are they who reach the farther shore.

But the disciples of Dhamma find Nirvana,
going beyond the difficult kingdom of death.

He gives up darkness and chooses light,
the wise man.
He gives up home, and desires to be homeless,
a hard choice.

Alone, single, casting away his pleasures,
he cleanses his heart—and rejoices.

Nirvana is his.
He knows the roots of knowledge.
His senses are well disciplined.
He is free from attachment.
He is radiant.

The Saint

No suffering for him
who is free from sorrow
free from the fetters of life
free in everything he does.
He has reached the end of his road.

He has no fixed habitation;
like a swan flown from its lake,
he is serious, he has left his home.

Like a bird invisibly flying in the sky,
he lives without possessions,
knowledge his food, freedom his world,
while others wonder.

Like a bird flying invisibly in the sky
while others wonder, he lives, the saint
without passions, indifferent to food,
aware of the meaning of freedom.

Even the gods envy him,
this charioteer saint who tames the horses of his senses,
yet is not proud.

He is like the earth, hospitable,
like a floor mat, submissive,
self-cleansing, like an unmuddy lake,
he is free from the wheel of birth and death.

He has found freedom—
peaceful his thinking, peaceful his speech,
peaceful his deed, tranquil his mind.

No one is higher than him,
who will not be deceived, who knows the essence,
who has abandoned desire, renounced the world,
and lives untouched by the flow of time.

Village or forest, water or land,
holy is the place where saints dwell.

Holy is the forest.
Holy is the place where the senses are at peace,
where the saint finds refuge and simple delight.

The Thousands

Better than a thousand vacuous speeches
is one sane word leading to peace.

Better than a thousand vacuous verses
is one sane line leading to peace.

Better than a hundred vacuous verses
is one sane truth leading to peace.

One man on the battlefield
conquers an army of a thousand men.
Another conquers himself—and he is greater.

Conquer yourself, not others.
Discipline yourself, learn restraint.

Neither a god, nor a gandharva, nor Mara
can topple the self-conquered man.

Month after month for a hundred years,
a man pays homage with a hundred sacrifices.
Another for a second honors a self-conquered man.
Consider him greater.

One man for a hundred years
performs the sacrificial fire in a forest.

Another for a moment honors the enlightened man.
Consider him greater.

A year's sacrifice, offering, or gift,
performed for the earning of merit,
is not worth a quarter of homage to virtue.

If a man honor the aged and practice faith,
four rewards follow: long life, beauty, joy, and strength.

One day of virtue and clear thinking is better
than a hundred years of vice and indiscipline.

One day of wisdom and clear thinking is better
than a hundred years of ignorance and indiscipline.

One day of effort and struggle is better
than a hundred years of sloth and weakness.

One day of insight into beginning and end is better
than a hundred years of ignorance about this.

One day of the experience of deathlessness is better
than a hundred years of ignorance about this.

One day of knowledge of Dhamma is better
than a hundred years of ignorance about this.

Evil Conduct

Move towards good. Cease from evil.
Evil takes over when good is neglected.

One evil is enough—why repeat it?
Only grief will follow if the mind thinks evil.

One good is a beginning which needs repetition.
Only joy will follow if the mind thinks good.

Happy is the sinner till evil ripens.
When evil ripens, he comes to grief.

Sad is the good man till good deeds ripen.
When good deeds ripen, joy surrounds him.

Some think lightly, "Evil won't touch me."
Evils fill a fool as drops fill a waterpot.

Some think lightly, "Virtues won't affect me."
Little drops fill a waterpot.
Little virtues make a wise man.

A rich and lonely trader avoids lonely dark roads.
A man in love with life avoids poison.
A wise man avoids evil deeds.

A finger without a wound touches poison,
and poison cannot harm it.
Evil cannot harm one who is not evil.

Like dust flung at the wind
which the wind flings back,
evil recoils on the fool
who harms the innocent.

The good go to heaven, the sinners to hell,
some are born again, and some find Nirvana.

Where in the world can a man escape
the evil results of his evil deeds?—
Not in the sky, not in the ocean,
not in the deep valleys of mighty mountains.

Where can a man escape death?—
Not in the sky, not in the ocean,
Not in the deep valleys of mighty mountains.

Punishment

All fear punishment, all fear death.
Therefore, do not kill, or cause to kill.
Do as you would want done to you.

All fear punishment, all love life.
Therefore, do not kill, or cause to kill.
Do as you would want done.

A man seeks his happiness and strikes with a stick
others who seek happiness just like himself.
He will not find happiness after his death.

Another seeks his happiness and does not strike others
who seek happiness just like himself.
He will find happiness after his death.

Speak gently, and they will respond.
Angry words hurt, and rebound on the speaker.

Nirvana:
When the agitated mind is as still as
a broken gong.

Like a cowherd with his staff pushing cattle into new pasture,
old age with death pushes the world's creatures into new lives.

How will a fool doing evil deeds know this?
He learns the hard way, burning in the fire of his deeds.

The man who punishes those who do not deserve punishment,
or offends the inoffensive, punishes and offends himself.

He suffers one of ten punishments:
grief, infirmity, disease, injury, insanity;

falling from royal favor, dreadful allegation,
loss of precious wealth, death of relatives;

or lightning falling on his house;
and when he dies, he goes to hell.

Sitting naked and still will not help,
matted hair, fasting, and dust will not help,
ash rubbed on body, lying supine will not help,
if the mind is not purified within.

What matters if he dresses well?
If his mind is serene, chaste, firm,
if he practices nonviolence,
he is the Brahmin, the ascetic, the bhikku.

Who is there in the world so chastened by conscience
that he never needs prodding?
For a good horse the whip is useless.

Be like the good horse,
swift, energetic when spurred.
Devotion, faith, knowledge, meditation,
energy and practice of the Dhamma
will set you free.

Planners make canals,
archers shoot arrows,
craftsmen fashion woodwork,
the wise man molds himself.

Old Age

The world is burning:
why is there laughter, why the sounds of joy?
Seek enlightenment, O fool,
for the darkness surrounds you.

Look at it—this painted shadow,
this body, crumbling, diseased, wounded,
held together by thoughts that come and go.

This body decays:
it is frail, diseases nest in it,
corrupt, it breaks into pieces,
it lives only to die.

And its bones are cast away
like seeds of watermelon in autumn.
Let him who will rejoice in this, rejoice.

Around these bones is built the fort,
mortared with flesh and plastered with blood.
Living in it are old age, death, pride, and deceit.

Like glittering royal chariots slowly rusting,
the body moves into old age.
"Only virtue is stainless," is the only wisdom.

A man who learns little grows old like an ox:
his body grows but his mind remains stagnant.

How many births have I known
without knowing the builder of this body!
How many births have I looked for him.
It is painful to be born again and again.

But now I have seen you, O builder of this body!
All desire is extinct, Nirvana is attained!
The rafters have crumbled, the ridgepole is smashed!
You will not build them again.

They pine away, the young men without discipline or struggle,
like old cranes starving in a lake without fish.

They lie like rejected bows, dreaming of the past,
these young men without discipline or struggle in their youth.

Your Self

Value your self, look after your self.
Be watchful throughout your life.

Learn what is right; test it and see;
then teach others—is the way of the pandit.

You are your own refuge;
there is no other refuge.
This refuge is hard to achieve.

One's self is the lord of oneself;
there is no other lord.
This lord is difficult to conquer.

Diamond breaks diamond,
evil crushes the evildoer.

As the creeper strangles the *sal* tree,
evil overpowers the evildoer.
His enemy could not be more delighted.

Easy to do an evil deed,
easy to harm oneself.
Difficult to do a good deed,
very difficult indeed.

Like the *khattaka* tree, dead after fruit-bearing,
or cut down for the sake of its fruit,
the foolish man sows his own destruction
by mocking the wise, the noble, and the virtuous.

You cannot save another, you can only save yourself.
You do the evil deed, you reap the bitter fruit.
You leave it undone, your self is purified.

Better is your own Dhamma, however weak,
than the Dhamma of another, however noble.
Look after your self, and be firm in your goal.

The World

Think clearly, avoid evil;
forsake false doctrine, deny the world.

Wake up!
There is no time to lose. Follow Dhamma.
The follower of Dhamma is happy now and forever.

Follow Dhamma, not the path of evil.
The follower of Dhamma is happy now and forever.

Say:
"The world is a bubble, the world is a shadow."
The king of death is helpless in the face of this wisdom.

Look!
The world is a royal chariot, glittering with paint.
No better.
    Fools are deceived, but the wise know better.

Like the moon slipping from behind a cloud and shining on the
  earth
is the man who, once foolish, has determined to be wise.

Like the moon slipping from behind a cloud and shining on the
    earth
is the man whose good deeds exceed his evil deeds.

Blind, blind is the world; only a handful can see.
Only a handful escape, like birds from a net.

Swans fly to the world of the sun,
all creatures that have power fly through the air.
The wise conquer Mara the temptress,
and escape from the world.

There is no evil that he will not do,
the mocker of Dhamma,
the liar, the scoffer of the other world.

Fools are not generous:
the world of the gods is not for the stingy.
Wise men are generous:
they find happiness in the next birth.

Better than lordship over the world,
better than going to the gods,
better than lordship over all the worlds,
is one step taken on the stream that leads to Nirvana.

71989

The Enlightened One

He conquers and is not conquered,
none in the world enters what he conquers,
he is the Buddha, the enlightened one,
infinitely aware, leader of himself,
impossible to describe in the languages of men.

No desires like nets trap him,
no passions like poison affect him.
He is the Buddha, the enlightened one,
infinitely aware, leader of himself,
impossible to describe in the languages of men.

Even the gods imitate wise men,
the enlightened, the dignified, the meditating, the free.

Hard it is to get born human,
hard it is to live like a human;
hard it is to listen to Dhamma,
hard to achieve the state of enlightenment.

Avoid evil, do good, cleanse your mind—
this is the teaching of the enlightened ones.

Be patient—long patience is high penance.
Nothing is higher than Nirvana.
No monk hurts, no ascetic oppresses another.

No malice, no injury,
disciplined eating and behaving,
high thinking and simple living—
this is the teaching of the enlightened ones.

A rain of gold coins will not quench passion.
The wise man knows, "Passions are passing and painful."

Divine pleasures will not quench passion.
Delight lies only in the destruction of desire.

Afraid, man runs to a place of safety,
to mountains, forests, sacred trees, and shrines.

Nothing is safe, not one of these is safe!
when he arrives there, his passions accompany him.

The only safety is the Buddha, the Dhamma, the Sangha,
the Four Noble Truths—the enlightened one knows this.

Suffering, the cause of suffering, the end of suffering,
and the noble Eightfold Path that leads to the end of suffering . . .

That is your refuge, that only is safe;
having reached that safety, all sorrows cease.

A noble man is hard to find.
The house where he is born prospers.

Blessed is the birth of the enlightened one,
blessed is the teaching of Dhamma,
blessed are they who make the Sangha,
blessed are they who live in harmony.

The man who respects those worthy of respect
(whether the enlightened one or his disciples),
those who have conquered and crossed the stream of sorrow,

The man who pays respect to those
who are free from the world, free from fear—
such a man's merit is measureless.

Happiness

Let us live happily,
hating none though others hate.
Let us live without hate among those who hate.

Let us live happily,
free from disease, among the diseased.
Let us live diseaseless among the diseased.

Let us live happily,
ungrieving among others who grieve.
Let us live without grief among those who grieve.

Let us live happily, without possessions.
Let us feed on happiness like the shining gods.

Victory breeds hate; the defeated will grieve.
Who goes beyond victory and defeat is happy.

No fire like passion,
no sickness like hate,
no grief like the ego's,
and no joy like peace.

No disease like greed,
no sorrow like desire.

He who knows this
is fit for Nirvana.

No gift like health,
no wealth like calm of mind,
no faith like trust,
no peace like Nirvana.

He who drinks from Dhamma
the sweetness of solitude
and the sweetness of serenity
finds freedom from fear and freedom from sin.

Living with fools is endless pain.
Better to live with an enemy instead.
Living with wise men, like living with kinsmen,
brings happiness.

Like the moon moving among star clusters,
one should move among the wise,
the holy, the faithful, the noble—
this is the essence of wisdom.

Pleasure

Who runs after pleasure and shuns meditation,
losing himself in the delights of the world,
envies the man who prefers meditation.

Give up both pleasant and unpleasant!
Missing the pleasant is pain, and
finding the unpleasant is also pain.

To lose what one loves is pain.
For which reason, control the senses.
Only he is free who neither likes nor dislikes.

Liking brings grief,
liking brings fear.
The man who curbs liking is free from grief
and free from fear.

Affection brings grief,
affection brings fear.
The man who curbs affection is free from grief
and free from fear.

Desire brings grief,
desire brings fear.
The man who curbs desire is free from grief
and free from fear.

Craving brings grief,
craving brings fear.
The man who curbs craving is free from grief
and free from fear.

Dear to the world is the man
who is truthful, virtuous, and discriminating,
who pursues his own business, which is devotion to Dhamma.

Only he crosses the stream of life
who wishes to know what is known as Unknowable,
who is lord of his senses and filled with dedication.

When, after a long journey a man returns home,
safely—kinsmen, friends, and well-wishers rejoice.

So, when a man travels from this birth
                    to the next,
his good deeds rejoice, waiting like kinsmen
                    to receive a friend.

Anger

Throw away anger, give up pride.
Give up worldly desires.
How can grief touch you
if nothing is your own?

Anger gallops like a wild chariot.
Hold it firm, steady it!
Be the true charioteer—
don't just finger the reins.

Be gentle with anger,
do good to evil;
be generous to the miser,
truthful to the liar.

Be truthful,
Curb anger.
Be liberal.
—Three ways to go to the gods.

Saints subdue their bodies,
saints injure nobody.
They find the eternal peace
in which is no grieving.

Those who are wakeful,
who study day and night,
who struggle for Nirvana,
find the eternal peace.

Tell me, Atula, who is spared?
"They blame the garrulous one,
and they blame the quiet one."
—An old truth, Atula, true even now.

There was never, there never will be, there is not now
a man for whom there is all blame, or all praise.

But the man who is known by those who know
to be spotless, wise, meditative, and virtuous,

He is like a gold coin found in the Jambu River.
Who dares blame him? The gods praise him, Brahma praises him.

Beware of the restless body.
Learn to discipline it.
Use the purified body to follow Dhamma.

Beware of the restless tongue.
Learn to discipline it.
Use the purified tongue to speak truth.

Beware of the restless mind.
Learn to discipline it.
Use the purified mind to practice virtue.

They are well disciplined indeed
whose body, speech, and mind are well disciplined.

Impurity

Here you are, a withered leaf,
waiting for the messenger of death.
You stand at the threshold,
unprepared for the journey.

Be a lamp to your self,
be like an island.
Struggle hard, be wise.
Cleansed of weakness, you will find heaven,
the land which few find.

Life is over, and you stand
       in Death's presence.
O unprepared for the journey,
       there is no rest on this road!

Be a lamp to your self,
be like an island.
Struggle hard, be wise.
Cleansed of weakness, you will find freedom
       from birth and old age.

As a smith removes flaws in silver,
a wise man removes flaws in himself,
slowly, one by one, carefully.

Iron breeds rust, and rust devours iron,
so ill deeds devour their doer.

As a house unrepaired decays,
goodness unrepeated declines.
Neglect of one's appearance decays it,
neglected, the mind stagnates.

Impure is the woman immodest,
impure the calculating giver;
impure are all evil deeds
now and forever.

But nothing is more impure, O bhikkus,
than ignorance.
Cast aside ignorance, and all becomes pure.

Life is easy for the shameless crow-strutter,
the mischief-maker, the minder of other people's business,
the insolent and the evil-minded.

Hard is life for the humble man,
hard for the pure, the clear-thinking,
the disinterested, and the gentle person.

Who takes life, tells a lie,
covets others' wealth, commits adultery,

And surrenders himself to strong liquors,
even in this world, digs his own grave.

Listen, O man!
Indiscipline begets evil.
Avarice and ill deed bring long misery.

Some give out of faith, others out of good will.
Forget the giving of others; or, day and night,
envy will oppress you.

Who forgets the giving of others
has peace of mind day and night,
because he has rooted out envy.

No fire like passion,
no jailer like hate,
no snare like delusion,
no torrent like craving.

How easy to see the faults of others—
we winnow them like chaff.

How hard to see one's own!—
We hide them, like cheating at dice.

How will he destroy his own passions,
who rouses them by watching others' faults,
who is forever finding something to condemn?

There is no path in the sky,
there is no refuge anywhere!
All is of the world, worldly—
only the Buddhas are free of the world.

There is no path in the sky,
there is no refuge anywhere!
Nothing in the changing world is unchanging—
only the Buddhas are free from change.

The Disciple of Dhamma

Force is not Dhamma,
> who uses it, not righteous.
Only he is wise
> who sees clearly before acting.

Nonviolence is Dhamma,
> who uses it, righteous.
He is Dhamma's guardian,
> he is wise and just.

Because he talks much
> a man is no pandit,
but because he is loving,
> fearless, and serene.

Because he talks much
> he does not know Dhamma,
but because he acts well,
> though his learning be little.

Because he has gray hair
> he is not an elder,
many put on ripeness
> and are not therefore wise.

Only he is an elder
 who is truthful and virtuous,
disciplined, nonviolent,
 innocent, and wise.

The man who is envious,
 evil, avaricious,
by good looks and loud talk
 cannot change overnight.

Only he who roots out
 these three great evils
can be said to be handsome,
 guiltless, and wise.

A liar with a shaven head
 does not make a monk.
How can a monk be
 restless and deceitful?

But the man in whom evil,
 small or big, has died out,
he is the true monk,
 subduer of his passions.

He who begs for alms
    is not the true bhikku,
only he who follows
    every word of Dhamma.

The man who is chaste,
    beyond good and evil,
who takes refuge in knowledge,
    is the true bhikku.

A fool will not be wise
    by holding his tongue.
The man who thinks clearly,
    examines good and evil,

And ends by choosing good
    is the wise man.
He has weighed what is thought of
    as worthy to be weighed.

It is not by hurting creatures
    that a man becomes excellent.
Only by nonviolence
    is excellence achieved.

Not by discipline or vows,
    not by great learning,
not by sleeping alone,
    not by serene meditation,

Will I find Nirvana.
    Work hard, O bhikku!
O bhikku, do not rest
    till all evils die out.

The Path

Of paths, the best is the Eightfold,
    the Four Truths are the best truths;
the best virtue is detachment,
    best among men he who follows Dhamma.

This is the path.
It leads to insight. It liberates.
Follow it.
Mara the temptress is helpless before it.

End your suffering. Follow it.
This is my path, preached
after the arrows fell away from me.

Work out your Nirvana with diligence.
The Buddhas only set examples.
Those who follow Dhamma and practice meditation
are freed from the traps of Mara the temptress.

Whatever consists of component parts must perish.
It is wisdom to know this.
This knowledge destroys grief and leads to liberation.

Whatever consists of component parts is full of grief.
It is wisdom to know this.
This knowledge destroys grief and leads to liberation.

Whatever consists of component parts is not the real self.
It is wisdom to know this.
This knowledge destroys grief and leads to liberation.

Wake up! It is time to wake up!
You are young, strong—why do you waver,
why are you lazy and irresolute?
This is not the way to wisdom.

Be strict with speech, control your mind,
let not the body do evil.
This is the way to wisdom,
these the three roads leading to it.

Meditation brings wisdom,
lack of meditation is folly.
These are the two roads,
one leading forward, one backwards.
Choose the right one,
the one that leads to wisdom.

Not one tree—cut down the whole forest!
There is danger in the forest.
Cut down the forest of desires, O bhikkus,
and discover the road to liberation.

Destroy the smallest desire for women!
It sticks one's mind to the world,
as a sucking calf sticks to its mother.

Take the ego like an autumn lily—
and snap it with your fingers!
Proceed then on the path to Nirvana
with one who has reached as your guide.

"This I choose for my winter home;
this for the monsoon, this for summer."
—The words of a fool.
He fails to see his final destination.

Like floods that come and sweep away a sleeping village,
death descends on the drowsy mind greedy for children and cattle.

Nothing saves!
Not father, not sons, not kinsmen.
They cannot save a man from death.

Therefore, think deeply.
Like the wise and virtuous man,
stay on the path that leads to liberation.

Varied Advice

Small pleasures given up for a larger joy—
this is the way of the wise, the far-seeing man.

Happiness for oneself by hurting others—
the way of the fool to get trapped in hate.

To-be-done discarded, not-to-be-done done—
the way of the wicked to increase his grief.

To-be-done observed, not-to-be-done discarded,
proper control practiced on the demands of the body—
the way of the thoughtful to end all impurity.

He kills his father and his mother,
he kills two Kshatriya kings,
he slaughters all the subjects of a kingdom—
and the saint unaffected proceeds as he is.

He kills his lust and ignorance,
he kills ambition and pride,
he slaughters all the evils of the body—
and the saint unaffected proceeds as he is.

The disciples of Gautama are always awake,
day and night thinking of the Enlightened One.

The disciples of Gautama are always awake,
day and night thinking of the Dhamma.

The disciples of Gautama are always awake,
day and night thinking of the Sangha.

The disciples of Gautama are always awake,
day and night thinking of disciplining the body.

The disciples of Gautama are always awake,
day and night delighting in compassion and love.

The disciples of Gautama are always awake,
day and night delighting in pure meditation.

It is painful to renounce the world.
It is painful to enjoy the world.
It is painful to be a householder.
It is painful to be unloved.
It is painful to be forever wandering.
O wanderer, wander no more,
suffer no more.

The man of faith is revered wherever he goes:
he has virtue and fame, he prospers.

Good men shine, even from a distance,
    like the Himalaya mountains,
but the wicked, like arrows shot in the night,
    fade away.

Sit alone, sleep alone, be active alone,
in loneliness continue the conquest of the self,
even in a forest continue the quest.

The Downward Path

The speaker of that which is not real goes down,
also he who, doing a thing, says, "I did not do it."
They are men of falseness;
after death, they are united, they become partners.

Many men dressed in saffron
    are ill-mannered and indisciplined;
the evil deeds of such evildoers,
    after death, drag them down.

Better for a boorish monk
    to swallow a red-hot steel ball
than in seeming goodness
    to live on people's almsgiving.

Four effects result from a fool's
    hankering for another man's wife—
much impurity, much restlessness,
    moral blame, the downward path.

Do not lust for another's wife.
    Much demerit follows, much punishment,
much fleeting and frightened pleasure
    in the arms of the frightened.

As a soft blade of *kusa* grass,
 wrongly handled, cuts the finger,
wrongly practiced, asceticism
 leads to the downward path.

Acts carefully performed,
 vows carefully kept,
reluctant practice of continence,
 do not bring rewards with them.

If a thing must be done,
 it must be done well!
A careless sadhu will find himself
 no cleaner than before.

Better an evil deed not done,
 than done, for future suffering.
Better a good deed done now,
 done, it brings no suffering.

A border post is well guarded,
 inside and out. Guard your self well.
Not a second must be wasted.
 Each wasted second makes a downward path.

Those who are ashamed of deeds
    that they should not be ashamed of,
and not ashamed of deeds
    they should be ashamed of—
such men follow false doctrines,
    and walk the downward path.

Those who fear when they should not fear,
    and do not fear when they ought to fear—
such men follow false doctrines,
    and walk the downward path.

Those who see evil where there is none,
    and see no evil where there is evil—
such men follow false doctrines,
    and walk the downward path.

Those who see evil where there is evil,
    and no evil where there is none—
such men follow the true doctrine,
    and walk straight.

The Elephant

I shall suffer hard words
    as the elephant suffers arrows in battle.
People are people,
    most of them ill-natured.

Only the tamed elephant goes into battle,
    the king rides only a tamed elephant;
he who tames himself is best among men,
    he suffers hard words patiently.

Tamed mules are excellent,
    Sindhu horses of good breeding, excellent;
excellent are elephants of war.
    Most excellent, however, is the self-tamer.

For no animals take one to Nirvana,
only the tamed self sees that untrodden land.

Consider the elephant Dhanapalaka,
    temples glistening with rutting juice;
restless, he does not eat,
    he pines for the elephant grove.

The glutton and the sluggard,
    lapped in foolish sleep,

like hogs wallowing in filth,
    find birth again and again.

There was a time when my mind wandered
    freely, doing what it pleased;
now I must rule it, like the mahout
    with his hook ruling the rutting elephant.

Check your mind.
Be on your guard.
Pull yourself out
as an elephant from mud.

If you have a friend sober, pure, and wise,
let nothing hold you back—
find delight and instruction in his company.

If you do not have a friend sober, pure, and wise,
walk alone—like a king who has renounced a conquered kingdom,
or an elephant roaming free in the forest.

Better aloneness than the friendship of a fool.
Walk alone like an elephant roaming free in the forest.
Be undemanding. Stay away from sin.

Friends give pleasure when needed.
Friendship is good when mutual.
Virtue's a friend when one dies.
Giving up sorrow gives virtue.

To be a mother is happy,
to be a father is happy.
It is happy to be a recluse,
it is happy to be a saint.

Happy is virtue that lasts,
happy is well-rooted faith,
happy it is to be wise,
happy to avoid sin.

Craving

Craving is like a creeper,
it strangles the fool.
He bounds like a monkey, from one birth to another,
looking for fruit.

When craving, like poison,
takes hold of a man,
his sorrows increase
like wild grass.

When this terrible craving,
fierce to subdue, is subdued,
sorrows slip off like
drops on a lotus leaf.

This is my advice:
"Root out craving! Root it out,
like wild grass is rooted out.
Do not let death destroy you
as river waters destroy reeds."

Like a tree recovering and growing
if its roots are not destroyed,
suffering recovers and grows
if craving is not conquered.

Thirty-six streams of sense flow in a man
looking for pleasure.
They seek passion,
their waves will sweep him away.

The streams are everywhere!
They flow everywhere!
Passion is everywhere!
Everywhere is the creeper!
Cut its roots with the help of wisdom.

Pleasures and affections are the lot of creatures.
Craving and fulfilling, the normal way.
Birth and old age are the usual fruits.

Crazed with craving,
men flee like hunted hares.
They are bound in chains,
they suffer again and again.

Crazed with craving,
men flee like hunted hares.
O bhikku, freedom comes only
from the conquest of craving.

Look at him!—
Having conquered the forest of desire,
he runs to the forest of new desires;
freed from the forest of desire,
he runs to the forest of new desires.
—All in vain; for he runs into bondage.

"Iron chains are strong,
there are wood fetters and fiber fetters,"
is wisdom, but wiser to say,
"No fetters like those of desire,
fetters of wealth, wives, sons,
fetters of consuming passion."

It is wisdom to say,
"Such fetters degrade, are hard to break."
Break them!
Renounce the world, discard desire,
forsake the pleasures of the senses.

Like the spider woven in its own web
is the man gripped by his craving.
Wise men renounce craving and leave the world,
wise men do not grieve, having discarded sorrow.

Give up what is before, what is behind,
Give up what is now, and cross the stream.
Then will your mind be free,
then will you cross birth and old age.

Craving grows
in a man restless, passionate, pleasure-seeking:
he strengthens his own fetters.

Who meditates quietly, discriminates,
and thinks of that which does not please the senses,
cuts the fetters of death.

The fearless, sinless, desireless man
escapes the thorns of life—this body is his last.

He is the great saint,
who quickly catches subtleties of words and meanings,
who is desireless, who knows what comes before what.
He is the *mahapurush*—this body is his last.

"I have conquered myself, I know all,
I am in all things sinless.
I have renounced all, I am free from craving,
I have no teacher, I have taught myself."

No gift is greater than the Dhamma,
no rasa sweeter than the Dhamma,
no bliss is greater than the Dhamma,
no conquest than being without craving.

Wealth hurts the foolish, not the seekers of Nirvana.
Who craves wealth destroys himself as well as others.

Weeds are the poison of fields
and passion the poison of man.
Honor the man without passion
and earn high reward.

Weeds are the poison of fields
and hate is the poison of man.
Honor the man without hate
and earn high reward.

Weeds are the poison of fields
and folly the poison of man.
Honor the man without folly
and earn high reward.

Weeds are the poison of fields
and desire the poison of man.
Honor the man without desire
and earn high reward.

The Bhikku

Control of the eye is good,
control of the ear is good,
control of the nose is good,
control of the tongue is good.

Control of the body is good,
controlled speech is good,
control in everything is good.
The self-controlled bhikku is the free bhikku.

He is the bhikku
whose hands and feet are controlled,
who is alone, serene, happy with himself.

How sweet the words of the bhikku
who, controlling his tongue, speaks wisely
of the Dhamma, in speech that is humble.

The bhikku who follows Dhamma,
delights in Dhamma, meditates on Dhamma,
does not stray from the true path.

What he receives, he takes humbly;
he does not envy others.
The envious bhikku is never serene.

Even the gods praise the bhikku
who takes humbly what little is given.
His life is pure and industrious.

He is the bhikku who owns nothing
as his, neither name nor form.
He does not grieve over that which is not.

That bhikku is tranquil
who has faith in the Dhamma.
Always gentle and equanimous,
he finds the holiest peace.

Make the boat light, bhikku!
Emptied, it will travel swifter.
Cast away passion and hate,
the road to Nirvana will be easier.

Cut off the five: egoism, doubt,
false holiness, lust, and hatred.
Destroy these five fetters,
and you will have crossed the stream of life.

Think, discriminate, bhikku!
There is no time to waste.

Forget the pleasures of the senses
lest, swallowing the flaming iron ball,
you cry out, "I suffer!"

How can one without wisdom meditate?
How can one without meditation be wise?
Both together, meditation and wisdom, lead to Nirvana.

When a tranquil bhikku enters an empty house,
he is delighted, if he has knowledge of the Dhamma.

When he realizes the birth and death of the body,
he is delighted, he experiences the delight of wisdom.

Let the wise bhikku begin thus:
controlling the senses, practicing equanimity,
following discipline as laid down in the Dhamma,
and choosing pure, noble, and industrious friends.

Let his life be a life of friendship.
Let him perform his duties well.
Then will his happiness end his suffering.

O bhikku, be like the *vassika* plant
that sheds its withered flowers.
Shed passion and hate.

That bhikku is calm
whose body is calm,
whose mind and speech are calı
who has single-mindedly
refused the world's seductions.

Rouse yourself by your self,
perfect yourself by your self.
Only such vigilance, O bhikku,
will bring you happiness.

You are your own refuge;
there is no other refuge.
Like the merchant taming a fine horse,
tame yourself, O bhikku.

Happy and peaceful is the bhikku
    who has faith in the Dhamma.
He alone finds the state of serenity
    where the world's flow ceases.

The young bhikku who ceaselessly
    follows the words of the Buddha,
he shines on this world
    like a moon escaped from cloud.

The Brahmin

Cross the stream, Brahmin, strive hard,
cast aside desire.
All that consists of component parts will perish.
Strive to know the imperishable.

When the Brahmin achieves full discipline and insight,
all fetters fall away.

Who is a Brahmin? I call him Brahmin
for whom is neither this nor the other shore,
who is free from the fetters of fear.

Who is a Brahmin? He is a Brahmin
whose passions are stilled, whose work is over,
who is taintless, meditative, and saintly.

The sun shines in the day,
the moon delights the night,
the soldier shines in his armor,
the Brahmin in meditation,
but the radiance of the Buddha
shines ceaselessly day and night.

He is a Brahmin who has cast aside evil,
he is an ascetic whose mind is equable,
he is a saint who has no impurity.

If attacked,
the Brahmin does not return in kind.
Cursed is he who kills a Brahmin,
more cursed a Brahmin angry with a sinner.

Highly regarded is the Brahmin
    who refrains from the pleasures of the senses.
Where nonviolence is practiced,
    suffering will cease.

Who is a Brahmin? He is a Brahmin
who is nonviolent in body, speech, and mind,
who has firmly controlled these three.

As a Brahmin worships before the ritual fire,
so should a man worship before one
who has understood fully the Dhamma of the Buddha.

Who is a Brahmin? I call him Brahmin
who practices truth and Dhamma.
Not matted hair, not noble birth,
not caste, make a Brahmin.
A Brahmin makes his own holiness.

Fool, what will matted hair do?
What will garment of goatskin do?
What use polishing the outside
if the inside is foul?

Who is a Brahmin? He is a Brahmin
who is lean and veined, solitary and serious,
who wears cast-off garments.

Who is a Brahmin? Not always he
whose mother is a Brahmin,
not he who is known to possessions,
but he who is detached.

Who is a Brahmin? I call him Brahmin
who is unshakable, fetter-free,
beyond attachment, separated from the world.

Who is a Brahmin? He is a Brahmin
who has cut the link, the thong, the rope,
who has broken free, who is fully awake.

Who is a Brahmin? He is a Brahmin
who, though innocent, endures mockery, insult, prison,
whose strength is patience, whose army is fortitude.

Who is a Brahmin? I call him Brahmin
who is never angry, who is pure and restrained,
who notes religious duties and follows moral rules,
for whom there is no rebirth.

Who is a Brahmin? He is a Brahmin
who does not cling to pleasures,
like a drop of water on a lotus leaf,
like a seed of mustard on the tip of an awl.

Who is a Brahmin? I call him Brahmin
who even in this world is free,
whose burden is ended, whose sufferings are over.

Who is a Brahmin? I call him Brahmin
whose knowledge is deep and wisdom profound,
who knows right from wrong, and has realized truth.

Who is a Brahmin? He is a Brahmin
who stays away from the well-housed and the houseless,
who does not live in houses, and has few wants.

Who is a Brahmin? He is a Brahmin
who does not use the rod to punish creatures
moving or unmoving; who neither kills nor conspires to kill.

Who is a Brahmin? I call him Brahmin
who is gentle among the aggressive,
peaceful among those with uplifted sticks,
detached among the attached.

Who is the Brahmin? He is the Brahmin
whose passion, hate, pride, and hypocrisy
fall away like a mustard seed from the tip of an awl.

Who is a Brahmin? I call him Brahmin
whose speech is truthful, soft, clear, inoffensive.

Who is a Brahmin? He is a Brahmin
who does not take what is not given,
long or short, big or small, good or bad.

Who is a Brahmin? I call him Brahmin
who covets neither this world nor the next,
who has no desires, who is separated from the world.

Who is a Brahmin? He is a Brahmin
who has no desires, whose doubts have been dissipated,
who has reached the final goal.

Who is a Brahmin? He is a Brahmin
who has gone beyond good and evil,
who has no sorrow, no passion, no taint.

Who is a Brahmin? I call him Brahmin
who is pure, serene, joylessly tranquil,
like the moon.

Who is a Brahmin? He is a Brahmin
who has crossed the mire of birth and delusion
(so difficult to cross) and reached the other shore,
who is calm, meditative, without greed, without doubt.

Who is a Brahmin? I call him Brahmin
who gives up sensual pleasures, wanders homeless,
and has renounced all desire for existence.

Who is a Brahmin? He is a Brahmin
whose passions are all conquered, who wanders homeless,
who has renounced all craving for existence.

Who is a Brahmin? I call him Brahmin
who has cast off attachment to things of the world
and to things divine, and has risen above both.

Who is a Brahmin? He is a Brahmin
who has renounced the pleasurable as well as the unpleasurable,
who is calm and unruffled, free from rebirth,
the conquering hero of the three worlds.

Who is a Brahmin? I call him Brahmin
who, knowing that things perish and are reborn,
lives nobly, feels purely, thinks clearly.

Who is a Brahmin? He is a Brahmin
whose ways are known neither to gods, spirits, or men,
who has exhausted his sins and become a saint.

Who is a Brahmin? I call him Brahmin
who has nothing, for he is unattached,
for whom is neither before, behind, nor between.

Who is a Brahmin? He is a Brahmin
who is brave as a bull, noble, wise, pure,
conqueror of death, the awakened one.

Who is a Brahmin? I call him Brahmin
who knows his previous births, knows heaven and hell,
is a saint with perfect wisdom,
and has done all that needed to be done.

SELECT BIBLIOGRAPHY

I. TRANSLATIONS OF THE "DHAMMAPADA"

J.A.: *The Dhammapada*. The Buddhist Society, London, 1945.
This readable "new version" is strongly recommended by Christmas Humphreys.

Anonymous: *The Dhammapada*. Theosophy Company, Bombay, 1957.
An Indian edition, reprinted with "the permission of the Cunningham Press in U.S.A.," the original publishers. Fluent and faithful.

Irving Babbitt: *The Dhammapada*. Oxford University Press, New York, 1936. Reprinted as a New Directions Paperbook, 1965.
Though this is stated on the cover to be "translated by Irving Babbitt," it is actually a revision of Max Müller's version of 1870. There is an excellent essay on "The Buddha and the Occident" added as an epilogue.

S. Beal: *The Dhammapada from the Buddhist Canon*. Trübner's Oriental Series, London, 1878.
A translation of the Chinese, not the Pali, text of the *Dhammapada*. Useful for comparative studies.

S. E. Frost, Jr.: *The Sacred Writings of the World's Great Religions*. The New Home Library, Philadelphia, 1947.
Contains long extracts from the *Dhammapada;* the editor does not mention the translator's name.

James Gray: *The Dhammapada*. London, 1881.
A workmanlike translation with an introductory essay.

Max Müller: *Dhammapada*. Oxford University Press, London, 1881.
The well-known translation by a careful German scholar, published in

the Sacred Books of the East Series, Vol. X. It has been reproduced, "with slight changes," in E. A. Burtt's *The Teachings of the Compassionate Buddha* (Mentor Books, 1955), in Clarence H. Hamilton's anthology *Buddhism: A Religion of Infinite Compassion* (The Liberal Arts Press, New York, 1952), in Lin Yutang's anthology *The Wisdom of India and China* (Modern Library Giant; also available as *The Wisdom of India,* published by Jaico, Bombay, 1955), and in Lewis Browne's *The World's Great Scriptures* (1945).

S. Radhakrishnan: *The Dhammapada*. Oxford University Press, London, 1950. Indian reprint, 1966.

A faithful and readable version containing useful introductory essays, the Pali text, and notes by a scholar of Sanskrit philosophy, now the president of India.

C. Kunhan Raja: *Dhammapada*. Theosophical Publishing House, Madras, 1956.

This somewhat heavy translation by a professor of Sanskrit contains an introduction in which Dr. Raja tries to "prove" the "Hindu" quality of Buddhism.

W. D. C. Wagiswara and K. J. Saunders: *The Buddha's "Way of Virtue."* John Murray, London, 1952.

A helpful, but uneven, translation by two members of the Royal Asiatic Society of Ceylon.

F. L. Woodward: *The Dhammapada*. London, 1921.

A verse translation recommended by Irving Babbitt.

There are in addition two well-known translations, one by Fausboll, who did the Latin version in 1855, and the other by Neumann, who in 1893 did the German verse rendering.

II. BOOKS ON BUDDHISM

G. F. Allen: *The Buddha's Philosophy*. Allen & Unwin, London, 1959.

Sir Edwin Arnold: *The Light of Asia or The Great Renunciation*. Routledge & Kegan Paul, London, 1891.

> A popular, and occasionally moving, account (in blank verse) of "The Life and Teaching of Gautama, Prince of India and Founder of Buddhism (As Told in Verse by an Indian Buddhist)." Victorian in style and outlook.

P. V. Bapat, ed.: *2500 Years of Buddhism*. Publications Division, Government of India, 1956.

> An extremely useful anthology of scholarly essays tracing the nature and development of Buddhism, this was published to mark the 2,500th anniversary of the Buddha's attainment of Nirvana.

Raghavendra Basak: *Buddha and Buddhism*. Sambodhi Publications, Calcutta, 1961.

L. Adams Beck: *The Life of the Buddha*. Collins, London, 1959.

E. W. Burlingame: *Buddhist Parables*. Yale University Press, New Haven, 1922.

E. A. Burtt: *The Teachings of the Compassionate Buddha*. The New American Library, Mentor Books, 1955.

> An excellent small anthology, with a lucid commentary.

Edward Conze: *Buddhist Scriptures*. Penguin Books, London, 1959.

> Other helpful books by this renowned Buddhist scholar are *Buddhist Texts Through the Ages* (Philosophical Library, New York, 1954), and *Buddhism: Its Essence and Development* (Harper, 1959).

Ananda Coomaraswamy: *Buddha and the Gospel of Buddhism*. Harper, New York, 1916. Harper Torchbook edition, revised by Mrs. Coomaraswamy, 1964.

Ananda Coomaraswamy and I. B. Horner: *The Living Thoughts of the Buddha*. Cassell, London, 1948.
An excellently organized selection from Buddhist texts, many of them obscure and previously untranslated. Another useful book by Coomaraswamy is *Hinduism and Buddhism* (Philosophical Library, New York, undated).

Alexandra David-Neel: *Buddhism: Its Doctrines and Methods*. John Lane, London, 1939.
A popular introduction; contains passages from the *Dhammapada* translated by Madame David-Neel.

Mrs. C. A. F. Rhys Davids: *Buddhism*. H. Holt & Co., New York, 1912.

T. W. Rhys Davids: *Buddhist India*. Putnam's, New York, 1903.

Sir Charles Eliot: *Hinduism and Buddhism,* 3 volumes. Routledge & Kegan Paul, London, 1921.
A comprehensive study by an acknowledged scholar; especially valuable for its critical examination of Buddhist philosophical ideas.

N. Gangulee: *The Buddha and His Message*. Popular Book Depot, Bombay, 1957.
An anthology of Buddhist texts, linked by a running commentary by a Bengali scholar. Introduction by Dr. S. Radhakrishnan; preface by Miss I. B. Horner.

Richard A. Gard: *Buddhism*. Washington Sq. Press, New York, 1963.
A painstaking account of Buddhist doctrine; contains excellent bibliographical references to out-of-the-way texts.

G. T. Garratt, ed.: *The Legacy of India*. Oxford University Press, London, 1937.

H. Hackmann: *Buddhism as a Religion*. Probsthain, London, 1910.

Christmas Humphreys: *Buddhism*. Penguin Books, London, 1951.
"The history, development, and present-day teaching of the various schools of Buddhism," presented lucidly by a devoted English Buddhist. An indispensable anthology by Mr. Humphreys is *The Wisdom of Buddhism* (Random House, 1961).

Nolan Pliny Jacobson: *Buddhism: The Religion of Analysis*. Allen & Unwin, London, 1966.
Contains a lucid essay on Buddhism by de la Vallée Poussin.

A. B. Keith: *Buddhist Philosophy in India and Ceylon*. Oxford University Press, London, 1923.

Henri de Lubac, S.J.: *Aspects of Buddhism*. Sheed & Ward, London, 1953.

E. F. C. Ludowyck: *The Footprints of the Buddha*. Allen & Unwin, London, 1958.

S. Luzanne: *Heritage of Buddha: The Story of Siddhartha Gautama*. The Philosophical Library, New York, 1953.

Kenneth W. Morgan, ed.: *The Path of the Buddha*. The Ronald Press, New York, 1956.

T. R. V. Murti: *The Central Philosophy of Buddhism*. Allen & Unwin, London, 1955.

V. S. Naravane: *The Lotus and the Elephant*. Asia Publishing House, Bombay, 1966.
> Contains a lucid essay on the life of the Buddha as revealed in legends.

John B. Noss: *Man's Religions*. Macmillan, New York, 1956.
> Discusses Buddhism clearly and in detail, but with a slight Christian bias.

Hermann Oldenberg: *Buddha: His Life, His Doctrine, His Order*. Williams and Norgate, London, 1882.
> A thorough and deservedly famous study by a German scholar.

S. Radhakrishnan, ed.: *History of Philosophy Eastern and Western*. Allen & Unwin, London, 1953.
> These two volumes were sponsored by the Ministry of Education, Government of India. The first contains three essays on Buddhism by Indian scholars.

Walpola Rahula: *What the Buddha Taught*. Grove Press, New York, 1962. First published, 1959.

N. Ramesan: *Glimpses of Buddhism*. Government of Andhra Pradesh, India, 1961.

Manmatha Nath Shastri: *Buddha: His Life, His Teachings, His Order*. Society for the Resuscitation of Indian Literature, Calcutta, 1901.
> Popular eclectic account of the Buddha's life and teachings; full of useful references to legend and history.

Anil de Silva-Vigier: *The Life of the Buddha Retold from Ancient Sources*. Phaidon Press, London, 1955.
> A sumptuously produced volume of photographs illustrating the Buddha's life; the introductory essay is in rich, lavish prose.

F. H. Smith: *The Buddhist Way of Life*. Hutchinson's University Library, London, 1951.

Bhikku Subhadra: *The Message of Buddhism*. Routledge & Kegan Paul, London, 1922.

E. J. Thomas: *The Life of Buddha as Legend and History*. Knopf, New York, 1927.

E. W. F. Tomlin: *Great Philosophers of the East*. Skeffington & Son, London, 1952. Arrow Books, 1959.
Helpful, readable account of the Buddha's life and his basic teachings.

C. H. S. Ward: *Buddhism*, Vol. I (Hinayana), 1947; Vol. II (Mahayana), 1952. The Epworth Press, London.

Henry Clarke Warren: *The Life of the Buddha*. Harvard University Press, 1922.

Max Weber: *The Religion of India: The Sociology of Hinduism and Buddhism*. The Free Press of Glencoe, 1962.

F. L. Woodward: *Some Sayings of the Buddha*. "World's Classics," Oxford University Press, London, 1925.

NOTE: The Associated Newspapers of Ceylon, Colombo, have published many books explaining the tenets and nature of Buddhism. Important among them are:
Mahathera Narada: *Buddhism in a Nutshell*
Thera Nyanaponika: *Manual of Buddhism*
Mahathera Nyanatiloka: *The Word of the Buddha*
Bhikku Dhammapala: *Basic Buddhism*